PROPERTY OF
ST. CLEMENT'S
LIBRARY
ROSEDALE, MD.

Look Before You Leap

Things to Know About Death and Dying

by

Lisa Ann Marsoli

SILVER BURDETT COMPANY
Morristown, New Jersey

Cincinnati • Glenview, Ill. • San Carlos, Calif. • Dallas • Atlanta • Agincourt, Ontario

Acknowledgments

The author would like to thank the following people for their guidance and helpful suggestions:

Harvey Abelman, school psychologist with the Board of Education in New York City for eighteen years, and therapist in private practice for fifteen years

Dr. Anne Fribourg, practicing psychologist for ten years, and associate of the Counseling and Psychotherapy Service of Greater New York

Dr. Bernard Starr, professor of developmental psychology at Brooklyn College's School of Education

Officer Pat Rodriguez of the Los Angeles Police Department

Mark Stevens, journalist with the United States Navy

Consultants

Sharon S. Brehm, Department of Psychology, University of Kansas

The Reverend W. Joel Warner, Chaplain's Office, Overlook Hospital, Summit, New Jersey

Credits

Cover illustration and design: Peggy Walker

Illustrations: Roberta Collier

Photographs: *Joanne Fink* 9; *Silver Burdett Company* 39, 40; *John Stevenson* 13, 18, 24, 27, 29, 30, 33, 36

Library of Congress Cataloging in Publication Data

Marsoli, Lisa Ann, 1958–
  Things to know about death and dying.

  (Look before you leap)
  Bibliography: p.
  Includes index.
  Summary: Briefly discusses many aspects of death, such as physical death, suicide, hospices, funerals, mourning practices, and obituaries.
    1. Death—Juvenile literature.   2. Death—Social aspects—Juvenile literature.   3. Death—Psychological aspects—Juvenile literature.   4. Funeral rites and ceremonies—Juvenile literature.   [1. Death]
I. Title. II. Series.
HQ1073.3.M37   1985   155.9'»37   84-40835
ISBN 0-382-06969-2 (soft)
ISBN 0-382-06780-0 (lib. bdg.)

Copyright©1985 Tribeca Communications, Inc.
Published by Silver Burdett Company
All rights reserved. No part of this book may be reproduced or utilized in any form, or by any means, electronic or mechanical, including photocopying, recording, or by any information storage or retrieval system, without permission in writing from the Publisher. Inquiries should be addressed to Silver Burdett Company, 250 James Street, Morristown, N.J. 07960

Published simultaneously in Canada by GLC/Silver Burdett Publishers.

Manufactured in the United States of America

Table of Contents

Introduction 5

Physical Death 6

Why People and Animals Die 7

    Death of Pets 8

Death Portrayed on Television. 10

Death of Relatives 12

Wills 15

Death of Children. 16

Suicide. 17

Wars 18

Memorial Day. 19

Dying in Hospitals. 20

Dying at Home or in a Hospice. 23

    Homes 23

    Hospices. 24

Funeral Ceremonies and Other Mourning Practices. . . .25

    Christian Ceremonies. 25

    Jewish Ceremonies 31

    Military Ceremonies..............................32

    Ceremonies for Police Officers and Firefighters......35

    Visiting the Gravesite............................35

Obituaries...36

Expressions of Sympathy.............................38

    Flowers...38

    Masses 38

    Donations.......................................41

    Memorial Funds 41

The Afterlife..42

More Information....................................43

    Places to Write 43

    Books to Read 43

Index...45

Introduction

Death and dying is often a difficult subject for people to think about. The idea of someone or something dying usually makes us feel sad. Even though death is a sad topic, it is an important one to explore.

At some point in your life a relative, someone you know, or a pet you own will die. When this happens, you will experience many different emotions, and not all of them will be easy to understand or deal with.

There are probably many questions about death and dying that you would like to have answers for. You may wonder why people and animals must die. You may want to know exactly what takes place in the body when death occurs. You may want to know about the many customs and ceremonies that take place after a person dies. You may have many different feelings about death, especially the death of someone you know.

This book will discuss all of these aspects of death and dying, and more. Talk to your parents or someone close to you about what you read, and explore your feelings about this subject together.

Physical Death

Death occurs when a person's respiratory and circulatory systems stop functioning. This means that a person stops breathing and blood stops flowing through the body. After a person or an animal dies, all parts of the body stop functioning.

Once people are dead, they cannot think, cannot feel pain, and cannot hear. When people die they no longer experience any of the things they could while they were alive. Death is final. Once people or animals are dead, they will always be dead.

Recently, some people have argued that a person is dead when their brain no longer functions. Even though their heart and circulatory system and lungs are still working, these people can no longer think.

Other people argue that such people are still alive. This argument is being discussed by religious leaders and medical authorities. The debate will probably go on for some time.

Why People and Animals Die

Everyone will die eventually. Death is a normal, natural part of life. Most people and animals die when they are old. They die because the organs of the body have weakened with age, and cannot function properly any longer or fight off disease.

Some people do not die of old age, but of illnesses. Sometimes, no matter how young or strong people are, a disease or physical defect can weaken them and cause them to die.

Sometimes people also die from accidents. They may be injured so seriously that they die instantly. Sometimes, even though a person's body continues to function long enough for medical help to arrive, they may be injured so seriously that they eventually die in spite of medical attention.

People also die in wars, and as a result of natural disasters like floods, tornadoes, or earthquakes. Others die because they are victims of crimes. You have probably heard about these kinds of deaths. You have seen them on television or read about them in newspapers.

Death is not a punishment. People do not die because of something bad that they did. Death is simply something that will eventually happen to every person and animal. If people and animals never died, the world would soon become overpopulated. There wouldn't be enough food for everyone to eat, or enough room for everyone to live.

Why do some people die when they are young, while other people die when they are old? What determines when it is someone's time to die?

Some people believe that there is a God who decides. They believe that death is a part of God's plan for their lives. Other people believe that no one decides, that death just happens. You will form your own opinion about why people die when they do based on your religious beliefs and family's teachings.

Death of Pets

You may now have, or may someday have a pet. You may have that pet for a long time. Pets do not live as long as people do though, and at some point your pet will die. It may die of old age, it may get sick, or it may be in an accident. It may be ill or in pain and have to be put to sleep by the vet.

Naturally, you love and care for your pet. You think of it as a friend. When your animal dies, you will feel sad and upset. These are normal emotions to have. You should expect to miss your pet. Often, people become just as attached to an animal friend as they do to a human.

As time passes, you will grow more and more used to its absence. Eventually, the time may come when you want to get a new pet. Wait and see how you feel.

When your pet dies, you should decide with your parents what you would like to do with its body. Discuss whether to bury it yourself, or let your veterinarian take care of it. If you decide to let your veterinarian handle it, you may want to find out exactly what will be done with the animal's body.

Regardless of whether you bury your pet yourself or not, you may want to have some kind of ceremony to mark its death. You may want to say a prayer, read a poem, or plant a tree or some flowers in its memory. A simple ceremony is a nice way to say good-bye to your pet.

There are special cemeteries where owners can bury their pets when they die.

Death Portrayed on Television

You may not get a very real idea of what death and dying is like from watching television. Often, television shows portray situations that don't usually occur in everyday life. In cartoons characters are run over and beaten up without ever getting injured. Actors on detective shows get shot or have car accidents and hardly get hurt at all.

On television, people who are supposed to be dying often look quite healthy. Someone may die on one television show and turn up perfectly healthy on another show a week or so later.

Of course, television shows are made up. The actors on them aren't really getting shot, aren't really sick, and aren't really dying. But people sometimes forget that what happens on television doesn't necessarily happen in real life.

When someone is shot in the real world, that person is likely to get injured seriously, or even killed. When a person is dying from an illness, they do not look healthy and perfect. Remember that most of what you see portrayed about death on television is not what actually happens in the real world.

Television shows may not give you a very realistic idea of what death is like.

Death of Relatives

At some point in your life, one of your relatives will die. The more important that person was in your everyday life, the greater the hurt you will feel when he or she dies.

You may have other feelings besides sadness when a member of your family dies. You may feel angry at the person who died for leaving you. You may feel as if the person has rejected or betrayed you by dying. You may feel guilty, too, thinking that you may have done or thought something which caused the person to die. Or, you may have done something or said something about the person just before they died. Little things may upset you, and you may have difficulty sleeping. These are all normal reactions to the loss of a loved one.

You must understand that nothing you can do or think can cause another person to die. You must also realize that when a member of your family dies, it is not to punish you in any way. You are not responsible for the death of your loved one.

Some children do not feel very upset when a member of their family dies. If you are like this, do not feel guilty because you are not feeling sad enough. Every person reacts somewhat differently to the death of a loved one. Even though you may not be overwhelmed by grief, this does not mean you did not love the person. Each person grieves in his or her own way.

Losing a member of your family is a difficult experience. Sometimes it helps just to talk about that experience with someone else. You may try to make it seem a little better by thinking of any positive aspects of the loss. If the person who died had been ill and in pain, remind yourself that death took that pain away. If the person who died was elderly, comfort yourself with the fact that he or she had led a long life. Although it may be hard to do, finding a bright spot in a sad occasion may provide you with some comfort.

People will try to comfort you during your time of mourning (while you grieve). Unfortunately, people don't always know exactly what to say or do to make you feel better. At times you may get angry with them and wish they would just leave you alone. It is all right to have these feelings. However, try to remember that your friends and relatives are just trying to help. They care about you and want to do all they can for you.

You will experience many different feelings when someone you know has died. People who care about you will try and comfort you. Don't be afraid to turn to them for help and support.

The death of any family member certainly will affect your life in some way. Some family members' deaths will affect you more than others. The bigger the part the person was of your everyday life, the bigger impact his or her death will have on you. It is for this reason that the death of a parent will bring the most changes to your life.

Obviously, you will go through many emotional changes if a parent dies. You will no longer be able to experience his or her love, care, and support. Your life may change in other ways, too. Your remaining parent will be busy trying to reorganize your household. You may have to take on additional responsibilities around your home. You may have to help take care of younger brothers and sisters. You may even have to give up some of your extra-curricular activities until your household gets back to normal.

Your family may move after the death of a parent. Your remaining parent may not be able to run the household any longer. Perhaps, he or she will want to move closer to relatives who can help take care of you. A move would bring even more changes to your life: a different house or apartment, a different neighborhood, a different school, different friends.

The death of a parent and all of the changes that come with it can seem overwhelming. Give yourself plenty of time to adjust to your new way of life. Don't be afraid to ask other people to help you get through this upsetting period. In time, you will laugh again, enjoy life again, and be happy again.

Wills

What happens to a person's possessions when he or she dies? People often have a legal document called a *will* drawn up by a lawyer which states who should get their possessions when they die. One person may be named to receive everything, or possessions may be divided among several people.

When writing a will a person usually includes the name of someone whose job it is to make sure the terms of the will are carried out. This person is called the *executor.* If there is no executor named, the court will appoint an administrator to fulfill the will's provisions. When people who die don't have wills, their belongings are usually divided among their closest relatives.

When people have children they often include a part in their will stating who they want to care for their children in the event of the parent's death. Parents may name members of the immediate family like grandparents or an aunt and uncle to care for the children. If there are no relatives who would be able to care for the children, then close friends of the parents may be named. If there is no will, children will usually be placed with relatives or friends of the family.

If there is more then one child in the family, every effort will be made to keep brothers and sisters together. When both parents die everyone's biggest concern is to place children in a home in which they will be loved and cared for.

Death of Children

When you think of people dying, you probably first think of old people. Old people are not the only people who die. Sometimes children die, too. They can die of many of the same things that adults die of.

Although it is not likely, you may someday know someone very young who will die. That person may be a member of your family, a classmate, friend, or neighbor.

The death of someone who is close to you in age may frighten you. It may make you feel afraid that you are going to die soon. Don't worry, the death of another child will not cause you to die young, too. His or her death will not put your life in danger.

If a child in your family dies, you may feel guilty that he or she died and you didn't. You may also feel that you caused his or her death. Try and remember that you have no control over another person's death. When it is someone's time to die, he or she will die.

Death is not always easy to understand. It is impossible to know why some people die when they do while other people continue to live.

Suicide

Suicide is a word used to describe when a person kills him- or herself. You may wonder why a person would *want* to die. Usually, people commit suicide because they are troubled inside. They may feel lonely or unloved. They may feel as if no one understands them. They may feel as if they have no one to talk to about their problems. To these people, death seems like a release from the emotional pain they are experiencing. Other people may commit suicide as a release from physical pain. They may already be dying, and are in such pain that they want to end their life quicker.

It may seem easier to accept someone's suicide when you know it was caused by physical pain. You can see when someone is suffering physically. Accepting someone's suicide when it was caused by emotional pain may be more difficult. Often, you cannot *see* emotional pain. You may not have realized how troubled the person was, so their death may come as a shock.

A person's suicide, like any death, may cause you to experience many different feelings. You might feel afraid, sad, angry, or guilty. Again, remember that you are not in any way responsible for that person's death. That person did not commit suicide to punish you or reject you. People kill themselves because of troubles deep within them.

If someone you know seems very depressed or upset, encourage them to talk to someone about what is bothering them. If someone you know ever talks about committing suicide, tell an adult whom you trust right away. If you ever feel this way, talk to your parents. If you feel you cannot talk to them, talk to another adult member of your family, a teacher, a member of the clergy, or some other adult.

Wars

War causes destruction—the destruction of human life, as well as the destruction of towns, cities, and countrysides. People who are in the military die in wars, and so do civilians. They are killed by bombs, bullets, chemicals, and other materials that can be used as weapons.

If wars cause people to die, then why do people get into them? People engage in wars for many reasons. They fight for land, they fight for religious freedom, and they fight for political power. Of course, there are other, more peaceful ways to solve problems. People can talk to each other to try and settle disputes. They can try to compromise so that each group gets some of the things it wants. Sometimes, though, people believe these methods will not work. They think that in certain cases war is the only way to solve problems. What do you think?

Monuments are often erected to honor those people who have died while defending their country.

Memorial Day

Memorial Day, also known as Decoration Day, is a holiday on which people remember the men and women who died in wars while serving in military forces of the United States. The first Memorial Day took place on May 5, 1866, in Waterloo, New York, when townspeople held ceremonies to commemorate the deaths of soldiers who fought in the Civil War. Over the past one hundred years, Memorial Day has evolved so it also commemorates the deaths of military personnel in the Spanish-American War, World War I, World War II, the Korean War, and the Vietnam War.

In 1971, Memorial Day was proclaimed a federal holiday by a law passed by the U.S. government. Some states celebrate Memorial Day on the last day in May, but the actual legal holiday is held on the fourth Monday in May. Some southern states also celebrate holidays specifically honoring Confederate soldiers who died in the Civil War. These days include Confederate Memorial Day, Confederate Decoration Day, and Confederate Heroes Day.

Many activities traditionally occur on Memorial Day. Military parades are held and ceremonies take place at monuments that honor the dead. People decorate the graves of people who have died in the military with flowers and American flags. In some places, tiny rafts or boats containing flowers and flags are set afloat in the ocean to remember military people who died at sea.

The main purpose of Memorial Day is to remember people who died while serving their country during a war. Over the years, this day has also come to be a time to honor all the dead.

Dying in Hospitals

Sometimes people become sick before they die. They may get an illness that is so severe their body cannot overcome it. They may stay at the hospital a long time—for weeks and even months. Someone close to you may someday become extremely ill, and not get better. He or she may stay at a hospital while dying. You will probably go to visit the person during that time. This may be a difficult experience for you.

It is strange to see someone you know in the unfamiliar surroundings of a hospital. The person may have tubes or needles in his or her body through which to receive medicine, or be hooked up to a machine to help in breathing.

He or she may not look like the same person you remember. People who are very ill often change in appearance. They may lose a great deal of weight, or become swollen. The color of their skin and eyes may change. Sometimes their hair changes color or falls out. These changes are sometimes due to the medication they are taking as well as their illness. Be prepared to see these differences in appearance when you visit.

Sometimes, seeing loved ones in the hospital makes it difficult to talk to them. You may feel uncomfortable because you are not used to being with them in this type of situation. The awkwardness you feel is often worse if the person you know is dying. Many people tend to be uncomfortable around individuals who are close family members or friends.

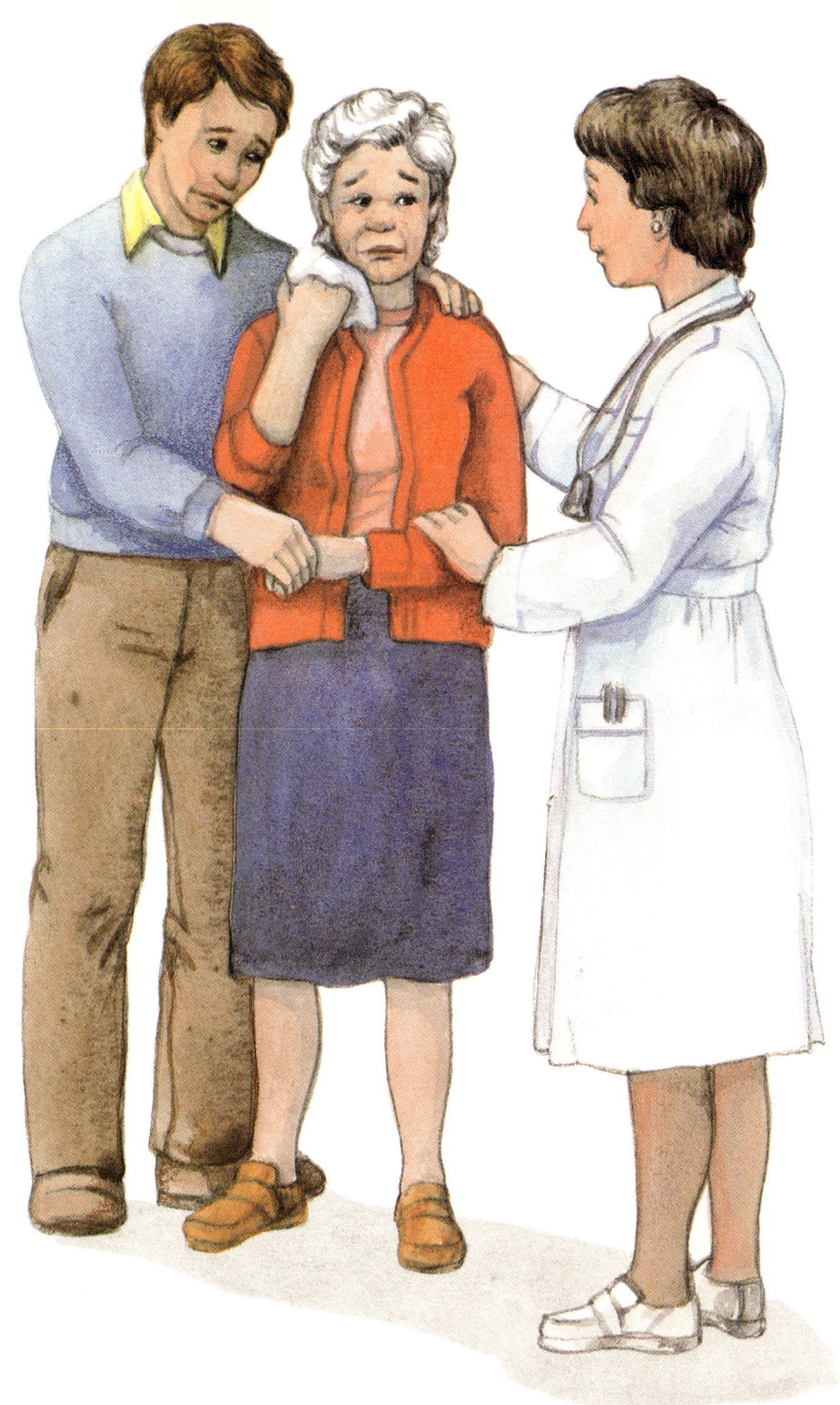

Many times people die in hospitals. Sometimes they have been sick for a long while, and in other cases only for a short period of time.

It may be difficult to know what to say to someone who is dying. Try not to feel awkward, simply talk to the person as you always have in the past. Remember that he or she is still the same person you have always known.

Sometimes people who are dying feel very alone. They feel as if there is no one who can possibly know what they are going through—and they are right. You can try and help them, though, by being as loving and supportive as you can.

Once you know that a person you care about is going to die soon, you should discuss how you feel with your parents, or some other adults that you know well. Talking about your feelings may help you to understand them better. Try and prepare yourself for your loved one's death by accepting the fact that it is going to take place. If you can face this very difficult truth, the shock will not be as great when that person does die.

People who die in hospitals haven't always been there for a long time before they die. They may have become ill suddenly, and been rushed to the hospital's emergency room.

It is always a shock when someone dies suddenly. You haven't had any time to consider that the person might die soon.

If someone close to you should die suddenly, be sure and talk to your parents or other adults about how you feel. Ask them any questions you may have about what has happened. Perhaps they can help you to understand the person's death a little better.

Dying at Home or in a Hospice

Home

Sometimes, people who are very ill do not stay in a hospital while they are dying. They will return home instead, where they have family and friends who will care for them. People may choose to stay at home for many reasons. The main reason is usually that they want to be in a familiar place, surrounded by their loved ones when they die.

If you ever live in a household with a dying relative you should expect some changes to occur in your daily routine. Obviously, having a very sick person around is going to change the way your family lives. The people responsible for most of the patient's care are going to have less time and attention to give to you. They may be very tired or irritable during this time. Your own routine will probably change a bit, too. For example, you may not be able to have friends over as often as you'd like.

Try and be as cooperative and understanding as you can. This is a difficult period for everyone. Pitch in and help care for the patient whenever you can. Read to the person, fill him or her in on what you've been doing, and just sit and talk. Don't make the person feel isolated from the rest of the family. Remember that a dying person has emotional as well as physical needs.

Even though life at home may change during this time, it doesn't have to become depressing. Do not feel guilty about playing or laughing or feeling happy just because there is a sick person in the house. Living in a sad atmosphere isn't going to do the patient, or the rest of the family, any good.

Discuss how the situation makes you feel with your parents or other adults. It might be a good idea to also spend time with friends, or an adult outside of the household. This will give you an opportunity to talk to someone who is not under the same stress as your family at home.

Hospices

Recently, special places called *hospices* have been established to provide places for people who have terminal illnesses and are dying. Hospices are like hospitals or nursing homes except they are set up to care for dying patients. The people who care for the dying are specially trained to cope with the physical and mental problems that the dying face. They also help the families and friends of the dying to come to grips with the patient's situation.

Hospices provide special care for terminally ill patients.

Funeral Ceremonies and Other Mourning Practices

When someone dies, there is usually some sort of funeral ceremony or other form of mourning held by friends and relatives. These practices have many functions. They establish a time for the dead to be buried or cremated. They acknowledge the sadness people feel over the person's death. They allow religious beliefs about death to be expressed. They provide a special time to remember the person who has just died. They also provide a time for mourners to gather together and comfort one another.

The family of the deceased (the person who has died) usually makes the decision as to what sort of funeral or other ceremonies to hold. They will base this decision on their religious or other personal beliefs. Sometimes people decide what kind of a ceremony they want before they die. If this is the case, the family will usually respect their wishes.

Christian Ceremonies

Christians usually hold what is called a wake. This is a time for visiting with the family of someone who has died. A wake is usually followed within the next few days by a funeral. At a wake, the body of the dead person is laid out in a coffin and displayed in a funeral home. During special viewing hours, people who knew the person can come and look at the body. Wakes are held so that people can publicly acknowledge their sadness over someone's death. It is also a time when mourners can comfort the dead person's family.

Funeral homes usually consist of several rooms. There are some rooms in which coffins can be displayed, and other rooms in which people can simply go to sit and relax. You will probably see many flower arrangements in the funeral home which have been sent by the friends and family of the deceased.

You may be asked to sign a special guest book which is usually placed at the entrance of the funeral home. This book is given to the family of the deceased so that they will know who came to pay their respects. Sometimes, when a very famous person dies, like the president of a country, the coffin is displayed in a public place instead of in a funeral home.

Before a body can be displayed in a funeral home, or other viewing place, it is usually prepared by the funeral home staff. The staff drains the blood out of the body and replaces it with a substance called embalming fluid. Embalming fluid contains chemicals that slow down the decaying process of the body. The staff will then dress the body in clothing provided to them by the deceased's family. They will also style the person's hair, and apply make-up to his or her face. After the body has gone through this preparation, it will be placed in a coffin which has been chosen by the family.

The coffin will be placed in one of the viewing rooms of the funeral home. There will be many chairs in the room facing the coffin. The lid of the coffin is divided into two halves. Sometimes the top half of the coffin will be left open so that the upper part of the body can be seen. Sometimes the coffin will be kept closed.

When someone dies a wake or viewing is held at a funeral home.

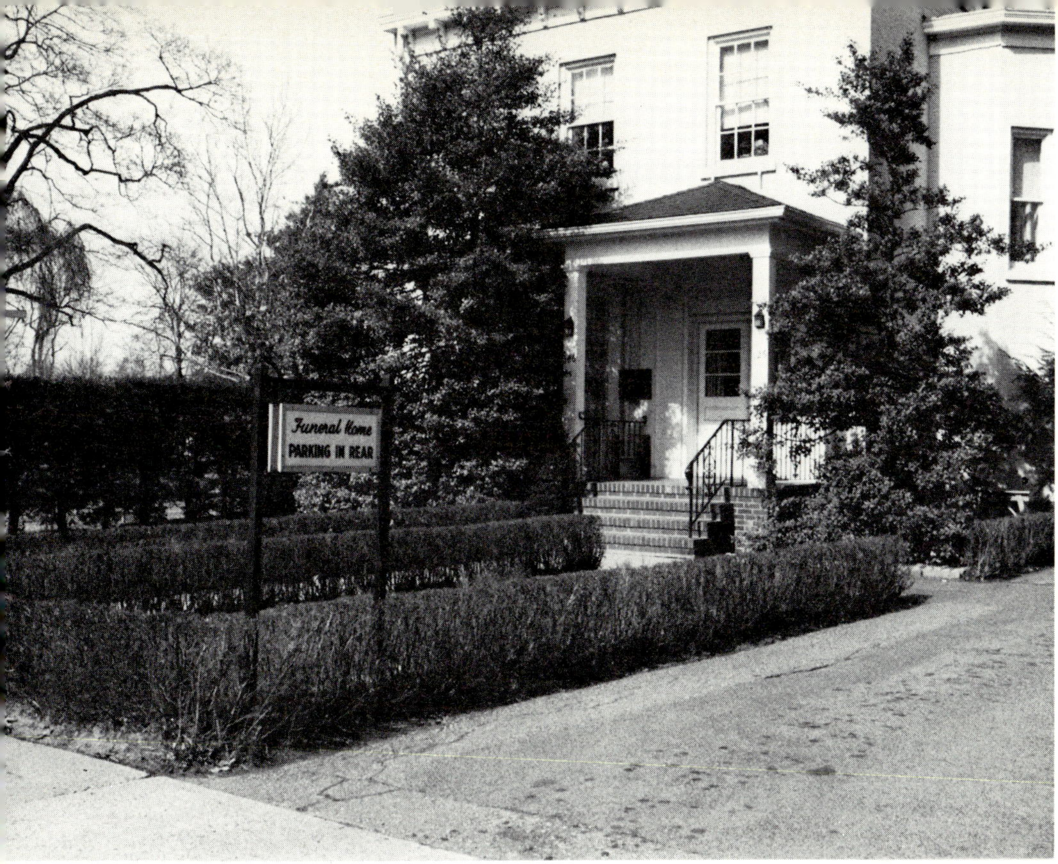
Funeral Home
PARKING IN REAR

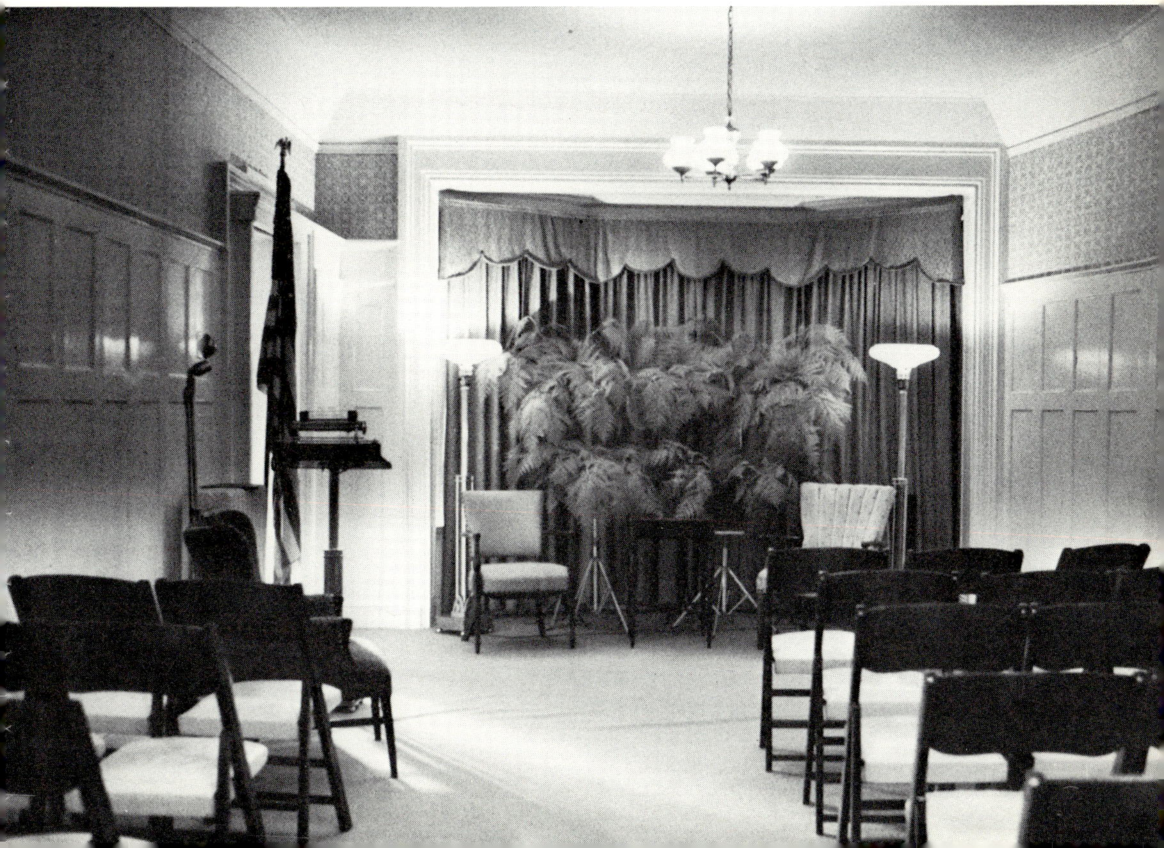

There is usually a small stool in front of the coffin on which people can kneel and pray. You may choose to stand or kneel close to the body, or to stand at a distance. You may or may not want to touch the body. Each person has his or her own feelings about this situation. Do whatever is comfortable for you. A wake or visiting hours may last from one to three days, depending on the wishes of the family.

On the last day of the wake, or the day after, a funeral is held. A Christian funeral begins with a religious service at either the funeral parlor or a church. If it is a church, the coffin will be transported there from the funeral home by a hearse. A hearse is a large car with room in back for a coffin. Pallbearers will carry the coffin from the hearse into the church. Pallbearers can be men who are relatives or friends of the deceased, or employees of the funeral home.

After the religious service, the coffin is taken back out to the hearse by the pallbearers. The hearse will be driven to the cemetery, and a row of cars containing the mourners will follow it. All of the cars will have their headlights on, even if it is daylight. This is a sign to other traffic to let the funeral procession through.

At the cemetery, the coffin will be taken from the hearse and brought to the gravesite or cemetery chapel. There, a brief ceremony will be held. Sometimes the coffin is lowered into the grave while the mourners are still present. If this is the case, members of the family may be asked to throw a handful of dirt or flowers on the lowered coffin.

A gravestone is usually placed at the head of the grave, though not always soon after the burial. The gravestone usually states the deceased's name, year of birth, and year of death. It may also have a prayer or poem inscribed on it as well.

After the funeral service the coffin is taken to a cemetery. There, a short ceremony is held, followed by the burial.

Not all coffins are buried. Some are placed in mausoleums. Mausoleums are buildings on the grounds of the cemetery. These buildings contain vaults in which coffins are placed. Large mausoleums have compartments in the walls that resemble drawers in which coffins can also be placed. The information about the deceased which usually appears on the gravestone appears on the outside of the vault or wall compartment.

Not all coffins are buried in cemeteries, some are placed in buildings called mausoleums.

Following the ceremony at the cemetery, the mourners often gather at the home of one of the deceased's relatives. There, they will eat, drink, and talk. This gathering gives everyone a chance to relax after the strain of the wake and funeral.

Sometimes people prefer to have a memorial service instead of a funeral. This is a time when people gather at a house of worship or other place without the coffin present. This service is held to remember and celebrate the life of the person who has died.

Jewish Ceremonies

Jewish mourning practices are a bit different from Christian ones. For example, wakes are not a part of the Jewish faith. Instead, the body of the dead person is buried as soon as possible after death. The burial usually takes place before sundown on the day after the person has died. The body is buried quickly to signify the mourner's love and concern for the dead. It also confirms their belief that even though someone has died, it is important for the living to continue with their lives.

A simple funeral ceremony is held at the grave, during which prayers are read. One important prayer that is said for the dead is *Kaddish*. This prayer is usually said by the children or siblings of the person who has died. Kaddish may also be recited by the family every day or every Sabbath for the year following the person's death.

For a week following the funeral a practice known as *sitting shivah* takes place. This is the time during which mourners go to the home of the family of the deceased. They bring food, and talk about the person who has died. In addition to remembering the dead, the mourners gather to comfort the family members who remain behind.

In the Jewish faith, several ceremonies take place to comemorate the one-year anniversary of a person's death. A gravestone is placed on the deceased's grave in a ceremony usually referred to as an *unveiling*. At this time, mourners again gather at the gravesite to remember their loved one. Other visits to the grave may be made by the family throughout the year.

Kaddish is said in the synagogue on the one-year anniversary of a person's death, and *Yahrzeit* candles are lit in the homes of the dead person's family members. These are special memorial candles which may also be lit on each annual anniversary of a person's death. On major religious holidays Jews also hold memorial services for all Jewish people who have died.

Military Ceremonies

A military funeral is held for someone who has died on active duty while serving his or her country. Military, police, and fire fighters' funerals are a little different than funerals for civilians. They are usually more formal and include special ceremonies to honor the deceased.

In the United States, there are four branches of the military—Army, Navy, Air Force, Marines. Each branch holds its own type of funeral service, but they are all quite similar to one another.

At a typical military funeral, the coffin of the deceased is draped with an American flag. The pallbearers at the funeral are uniformed officers belonging to the same branch of the military as the deceased. If the family wishes, a military chaplain will perform the funeral services at the church, chapel, temple, or gravesite.

People who have served in the military can be buried in military cemeteries if they so choose.

33

During the burial, one or more color guards will be present. Color guards are members of the military who wear special dress uniforms. Their presence at a ceremony is a sign of honor toward the deceased. At some stage during the graveside service, the color guard folds the flag on the coffin in a special way and presents it to the family of the dead person.

A bugler is also present who plays "taps", a bugle call traditionally played at military funerals. There may be a gun salute as well, during which uniformed military personnel fire blanks from their rifles.

At some Air Force funerals, Air Force jets fly overhead in formation as another sign of respect for the deceased. All military personnel who die while on active duty can be buried in a national cemetery if their families so desire.

In addition to military funerals held on land, the Navy also performs burials at sea. For this ceremony, the deceased's body is placed on a Navy ship in a weighted gunney sack or metal casket. The sack or casket is draped with an American flag. The family of the deceased, a bugler, a military chaplain, a photographer, and other Navy personnel are also on board.

The ship goes out to sea, and a spot is chosen for burial. The flag is folded and given to the deceased's family. The bugler plays "taps" and the gunney sack or coffin is lowered off the ship into the sea. The photographer takes pictures of the burial, which will later be given to the deceased's family. They will also be given a map showing exactly where the body was placed in the sea.

Ceremonies For Police Officers and Firefighters

The funerals held for police officers and firefighters are similar to military funerals in many ways. The coffin is covered with an American flag which is presented to the family before burial. All officers attending the ceremonies are in uniform. A color guard is present, as well as a department chaplain, who may perform the funeral services if the family wishes. The chief of police or fire chief usually attends the services, and the governor or mayor sends certificates of honor to be presented to the family.

These funerals also include a motorcade which accompanies the hearse from the funeral home to the cemetery. For a police funeral uniformed members of the department ride in police cars and on police motorcycles to the front, back, and sides of the hearse with their headlights on and red lights turning. Usually, the funerals of high ranking government officials will also include police motorcades, and other honors such as gun salutes and color guards.

Visiting the Gravesite

People often visit the grave or mausoleum of a loved one long after the funeral ceremonies have taken place. How often someone will visit depends on the individual. Some people will visit regularly, others only on special occasions and holidays, and some do not visit at all.

Relatives and friends who do visit will often leave flowers or plants at the mausoleum or gravesite. They may even plant flowers at the grave. They may say prayers at the cemetery, or simply think about the person who has died. Making trips to the grave or mausoleum of a loved one is one way that people remember the dead.

When someone close to you dies, should you attend the ceremonies that follow? Decide how you feel. Now that you know what the different ceremonies consist of, the decision to go or not may be a bit easier to make. Discuss your feelings with parents or other adults you feel close to. Do not feel badly if you decide not to attend any of the funeral services. You are free to mourn in whatever way is best for you. If you do choose to attend funeral services, be sure to ask adults any questions you may have, before or after the services.

Relatives and friends often make visits to the gravesite. They may leave flowers or say prayers to remember the person who has died.

Obituaries

An obituary is an announcement of someone's death. Obituaries are published in a special section of the newspaper. They contain information about the dead person and details about their funeral arrangements. Obituaries may include all or some of the following information.

- name of the deceased

- date of death

- name of hometown

- place of death

- age

- names of surviving family members

- schools attended

- military service

- funeral home where viewing will be held

- date and time of viewing

- where and when funeral services will be held

- place where donations may be sent

Expressions of Sympathy

Friends and relatives of the deceased and their family often like to do something to show their concern. The simplest way to let the family know you are thinking of them is to send a sympathy card. Others may decide to write a letter or short note. Some people, who are perhaps closer to the deceased or the family, often want to do more to show their sympathy, and pay tribute to the person who has died. There are many ways in which this can be done. These gestures include sending flowers, making a donation to a charitable organization of some sort, having a mass said in the person's memory, or establishing a memorial fund.

Flowers

Flowers are the most traditional way of paying tribute to the deceased. It has been a long-time custom to have floral arrangements sent to the funeral home. They are displayed there during the wake, near the coffin. After the wake is over they are transported to the burial site and left by the grave.

Masses

Saying masses in memory of the deceased is another way to pay tribute. Arrangements can be made with the church pastor to have one of the weekly or Sunday masses said for the deceased. You and the pastor select the time and date of the mass. The pastor enters this information on a *mass card* which can be mailed or presented to the family.

A mass card is given to the family of the deceased when a mass is to be said in that person's memory.

he who follows Me does not walk in darkness but will have the **Light of Life**

The Holy Sacrifice of the Mass will be offered for the repose of the soul of

Caroline M. Woods

Rev. Michael McGuire
Church of the Assumption
91 Maple Avenue
Morristown, N.J. 07960

Date May 15, 1985
Time 10:30 AM

With the sympathy of

Mr & Mrs. Henry Thompson

In memory of
James B. Davis
The American Cancer Society
has received a gift from
Richard and Nancy Rowen

IN MEMORIAM

Donations to a charity are a way many people pay tribute to someone who has died.

Donations

Recently, people seem to be moving away from the custom of sending flowers. Many people feel that making a donation in the dead person's memory is a more practical way of paying tribute. Flowers die, but a donation to a charity, research group, school, or foundation can be put to a variety of good uses and has a more lasting effect.

Often, the family will specify in the obituary that instead of flowers they would like to have donations made to a certain organization. Frequently, if the death was caused by a specific illness (cancer, heart disease, leukemia), it will be requested that any donations be made to the foundation that conducts research for that disease (The American Cancer Society, The American Heart Association, The National Leukemia Foundation).

Some people request that a contribution be made to a favorite charity—The Humane Society, Easter Seals, or March of Dimes, just to name a few. Others like to have contributions made to the college or university they attended, a volunteer fire department or ambulance corps, or a hospital.

The organizations that receive these donations acknowledge them by sending the family a notice of some sort. This notice states that a contribution has been made by a certain individual in memory of the deceased.

Memorial Funds

Frequently, when a police officer or firefighter dies, the department they were a member of sets up a memorial fund. The money that people donate to the fund is generally presented to the family to help bear the funeral costs, to help support the family, or as an educational fund for the children.

The Afterlife

Many people believe that a person has not only a physical body, but a spiritual body as well. The spiritual part is referred to as the *soul*. These people believe that when a person dies, the soul continues to exist. The term *afterlife* refers to what happens to the soul after a person dies. Each person who believes in an afterlife has his or her own idea of what it is like.

You have heard of the concepts of Heaven and Hell. Many people believe that Heaven is where God lives, and Hell is thought to be a place where God is absent. When someone dies, people who believe in this type of afterlife pray that the dead person's soul will go to Heaven. They believe that there it will exist in peace.

Other people do not believe in an afterlife. They believe that when someone dies, their entire being is dead, except for the memories of them that remain with those who are still living. Still, what happens when someone dies is something that no one can say for sure. Once someone dies, that person cannot come back and tell the living what death is like. The living must rely on their hearts and minds to tell them what to believe.

You may have your own beliefs about what happens to someone when he or she dies. Maybe you haven't decided what you think yet. Your ideas about this may change many times throughout your life. It is good to talk about both your beliefs and your doubts with someone you trust, like your parents, a teacher, or a member of the clergy.

More Information

Places to Write

If you or your family need help dealing with the death of a loved one, write or call:

> COMPASSIONATE FRIENDS
> P.O. Box 1347
> Oakbrook, Illinois 60521
> (312) 323-5010

Books to Read

Here is a list of other books about death and dying you might find interesting:

Non-fiction

LEARNING TO SAY GOOD-BY WHEN A PARENT DIES
by Eda LeShan
Published by Macmillan Publishing Company, Inc. in 1976

LIFE AND DEATH
By Herbert Spencer Zim and Sonia Bleecker
Published by William Morrow & Company in 1970

HOW IT FEELS WHEN A PARENT DIES
by Jill Krementz
Published by Alfred A. Knopf in 1981

Fiction

GROVER
by Vera and Bill Cleaver
Published by J.B. Lippincott Company in 1970

HANG TOUGH, PAUL MATHER
by Alfred Slote
Published by J.B. Lippincott Company in 1973

A SUMMER TO DIE
by Lois Lowry
Published by Houghton Mifflin Company in 1977

THERE ARE TWO KINDS OF TERRIBLE
by Peggy Mann
Published by Doubleday & Company, Inc. in 1977

WHAT HAPPENED WHEN GRANDMA DIED (Christian)
by Peggy Barker
Published by Doubleday & Company, Inc. in 1984

INDEX

afterlife • 42

brain death • 6

cemeteries • 28–33

children, death of • 16

Christian mourning practices • 25–31

coffins • 26–28

custody • 15

death portrayed on television • 10–11

donations • 40–41

firefighters' funerals • 35

flowers • 38

funerals • 25–35

graveside ceremonies • 28–30

gravestones • 28, 32

hearses • 28

Heaven • 42

Hell • 42

home, death in the • 23–24

hospices • 24

hospitals, death in • 20–22

Jewish mourning practices • 31–32

Kaddish • 31

masses • 38

mass cards • 38

mausoleums • 30

Memorial Day • 19

memorial funds • 41

military funerals • 32–33

obituaries • 36

pallbearers • 28

parents, death of • 12–15

pets • 8–9

physical death • 6

police funerals • 35

reasons for death • 7

relatives, death of • 12–15

(sitting) shivah • 32

souls • 41

suicide • 17

sympathy cards • 38

viewings • 25–26

wakes • 25–28

wars • 18

wills • 15

Sources

Corr, Charles A. and Hannelore Wass, eds. HELPING CHILDREN COPE WITH DEATH, second edition. New York: Hemisphere Publishing Corporation, 1982.

Epstein, Morris. ALL ABOUT JEWISH HOLIDAYS AND CUSTOMS. New York: Ktav Publishing House, Inc., 1970.

Jackson, Edgar N., TELLING A CHILD ABOUT DEATH. New York: Channel Press, 1965.

Kellerman, Dr. Jonathan. HELPING THE FEARFUL CHILD: A GUIDE TO EVERYDAY AND PROBLEM ANXIETIES. New York: W.W. Norton & Company, 1981.

Kubler-Ross, Dr. Elisabeth. ON CHILDREN AND DEATH. New York: Macmillan Publishing Company, Inc., 1983.

Kubler-Ross, Dr. Elisabeth. QUESTIONS AND ANSWERS ON DEATH AND DYING. New York: Macmillan Publishing Company, Inc., 1974.

Kubler-Ross, Dr. Elisabeth, ed. DEATH: THE FINAL STAGE OF GROWTH. Englewood Cliffs, New Jersey: Prentice-Hall, Inc., 1975.

Kubler-Ross, Dr. Elisabeth, ed. LIVING WITH DEATH AND DYING. New York: Macmillan Publishing Company, Inc., 1981.

MERIT STUDENT'S ENCYCLOPEDIA, Vol. 19. New York: Macmillan Educational Corporation and P.F. Collier, Inc., 1978.

Pattison, E. Mansell, ed. THE EXPERIENCE OF DYING. Englewood Cliffs, New Jersey: Prentice-Hall, Inc., 1977.

Shneidman, Edwin S., Ph.D., ed. DEATH: CURRENT PERSPECTIVES, third edition. Palo Alto, California: Mayfield Publishing Company, 1984.

Simos, Bertha G. A TIME TO GRIEVE—LOSS AS A UNIVERSAL HUMAN EXPERIENCE. New York: Family Service Association of America, 1979.

THE WORLD BOOK ENCYCLOPEDIA, Vol. 13. Chicago: World Book, Inc., 1984.